MY FIRST
FIND OUT
ABOUT BOOK

People Jesus Met

MY FIRST
FIND OUT
ABOUT BOOK

People Jesus Met

Stephanie Jeffs
and Jenny Tulip

LOYOLAPRESS.
CHICAGO

Jesus and his friends

"Follow me," called Jesus.
"Help me tell everyone about God."

Simon Peter and Andrew were fishermen.
They left their nets by the Sea of Galilee.

James and his brother John left their boats.

Matthew, the tax collector, left his job.

Then Philip, Bartholomew, Thomas, James,
Simon, Thaddeus and Judas Iscariot
all decided to follow Jesus, too.

They became Jesus' special friends.

How many special friends did Jesus have?

The friends who helped

Once there was a man who couldn't walk.
He was so sick he couldn't move at all.
His friends carried him to Jesus.

The house was full of people.
So the friends carried the man up to the roof.
Then they made a hole in the roof and
lowered the man down to Jesus.

When Jesus saw the man he said,
"You can get up and go home!"
Jesus had made the man well!
The man got up and walked out of the house.
Everyone was amazed and thanked God.

Point to the sick man's friends.

Jesus and the Roman soldier

One day a Roman soldier came to Jesus.
"Please help me, Jesus," he said.
"My dear servant is very sick in bed."

"I will go and make him better," promised Jesus.

"No," said the soldier. "You do not need to come to my house. Just say so, and he will be better."

Jesus was surprised.
"You are a good man of faith," he said.
"Go home, and your servant will be better."
The Roman soldier went home very happy
and found his dear servant completely well.

How many Roman soldiers can you see?

Jesus heals a little girl

Jairus was a very important man.
He rushed through the crowd, looking for Jesus.

"Please come to my house," he begged.
"My little girl is very ill."
But when Jesus reached the house,
the little girl had died.

Jesus went inside with Simon Peter, James, and John.
He held the little girl's hand.
"Little girl, get up now," he said.

The little girl stood up.
Jesus had made her well again!

Find Jesus and the little girl.

Jesus and the two sisters

Mary and Martha were very excited.
Jesus and his friends were coming to stay.
There was so much to get ready!

Martha was still busy when Jesus arrived.
But Mary didn't do anything to help!
She sat and listened to Jesus.

Martha was angry. "It's not fair!" she said.
"Tell Mary to help me."

"Martha," said Jesus kindly.
"Mary is doing the right thing.
Let's be together while we can."

What food can you see on the table?

The very rich man

One day a rich man came to see Jesus.
"Tell me how I can please God," he said.

"Obey him," replied Jesus.
"I have done that," said the man.
"There's one thing more," said Jesus.
"Give away all your money.
Come with me to tell people about God."

The man was sad. He was very, very rich.
He walked away from Jesus and went home.
Jesus was sad too.
He knew the man loved his money more than God.

What is the man wearing that shows he is rich?

The ten men on the road

Jesus was going to Jerusalem with his friends.
On the road he met ten men.
They had an illness which made their skin sore.
Nobody wanted to be with them.

"Jesus, help us! Make us better!" they shouted.

"Walk to the village and you will be better," said Jesus.

The men walked to the village and when they got there,
they were all better.
One of them ran back to Jesus right away.
"Thank you, Jesus!" he said.

Where are the nine men who forgot to say
thank you?

Jesus meets Bartimaeus

Bartimaeus was blind.
One day he heard that Jesus was coming.

"Jesus, help me!" he called.
"Be quiet!" someone shouted back unkindly.
But Jesus heard Bartimaeus.
"Come here!" he said.

Bartimaeus stood up and felt his way to Jesus.
"How can I help you?" asked Jesus.
"I know you can make me see," said Bartimaeus.

Suddenly Bartimaeus could see.
He followed Jesus joyfully.

Can you find the cloak, begging bowl, and stick that
Bartimaeus dropped on the ground?

The little tax collector

One day crowds of people came to see Jesus.
Zacchaeus was too small to see anything,
so he climbed a fig tree.

No one liked Zacchaeus.
He was rich because he cheated people
when he collected the taxes.

"Come down," said Jesus.
"I'm staying at your house today."

After that, Zacchaeus stopped cheating.
He gave back the money he had taken.
He became a friend of Jesus.

Find three people standing on the roofs
of their houses.

Jesus and the little children

Jesus' friends were fed up.
Crowds of people had brought their children
to see Jesus.

"Go away!" said Jesus' friends angrily.

"You must not say that!" said Jesus.
"I want the children to come to me.
God loves every single one of them."

The children ran to Jesus.
He picked them up and blessed them.
Jesus loved the children, and they loved him.

What toys can you see in the picture?

First published in North America in 2001 by

LOYOLAPRESS.
CHICAGO

3441 N Ashland Ave
Chicago, Illinois 60657

ISBN 0-8294-1731-1

Original edition published in 2000 in the UK by The Bible Reading Fellowship

Copyright © 2000 AD Publishing Services Ltd
1 Churchgates, The Wilderness, Berkhamsted, Herts HP4 2UB
Illustrations copyright © 2000 Jenny Tulip

Bible stories can be found as follows:
Jesus and his friends: Mark 1:16–20; Mark 2:13–17
The friends who helped: Mark 2:1–12
Jesus and the Roman soldier: Matthew 8:5–13
Jesus heals a little girl: Mark 5:21–42
Jesus and the two sisters: Luke 10:38–42
The very rich man: Mark 10:17–31
The ten men on the road: Luke 17:11–19
Jesus meets Bartimaeus: Mark 10:46–52
The little tax collector: Luke 19:1–9
Jesus and the little children: Mark 10:13–16

Printed and bound in Hong Kong